Beetles

by Grace Hansen

ABDO
INSECTS
Kids

www.abdopublishing.com

Published by Abdo Kids, a division of ABDO, P.O. Box 398166, Minneapolis, Minnesota 55439.

Printed in the United States of America, North Mankato, Minnesota.

052014

092014

 **THIS BOOK CONTAINS
RECYCLED MATERIALS**

Photo Credits: Shutterstock, Thinkstock

Production Contributors: Teddy Borth, Jennie Forsberg, Grace Hansen

Design Contributors: Candice Keimig, Laura Rask, Dorothy Toth

Library of Congress Control Number: 2013952084

Cataloging-in-Publication Data

Hansen, Grace.
 Beetles / Grace Hansen.
   p. cm. -- (Insects)
ISBN 978-1-62970-038-0 (lib. bdg.)
Includes bibliographical references and index.
1. Beetles--Juvenile literature.   I. Title.
595.76--dc23
                     2013952084

Table of Contents

Beetles

Beetles are insects. Ants, bees, and butterflies are all insects too.

Beetles can be found almost

everywhere on Earth. They

live on land and in fresh water.

7

Most beetles are black or brown. Some beetles can be very colorful.

9

Beetles have three main body
parts. They are the head,
thorax, and the **abdomen**.

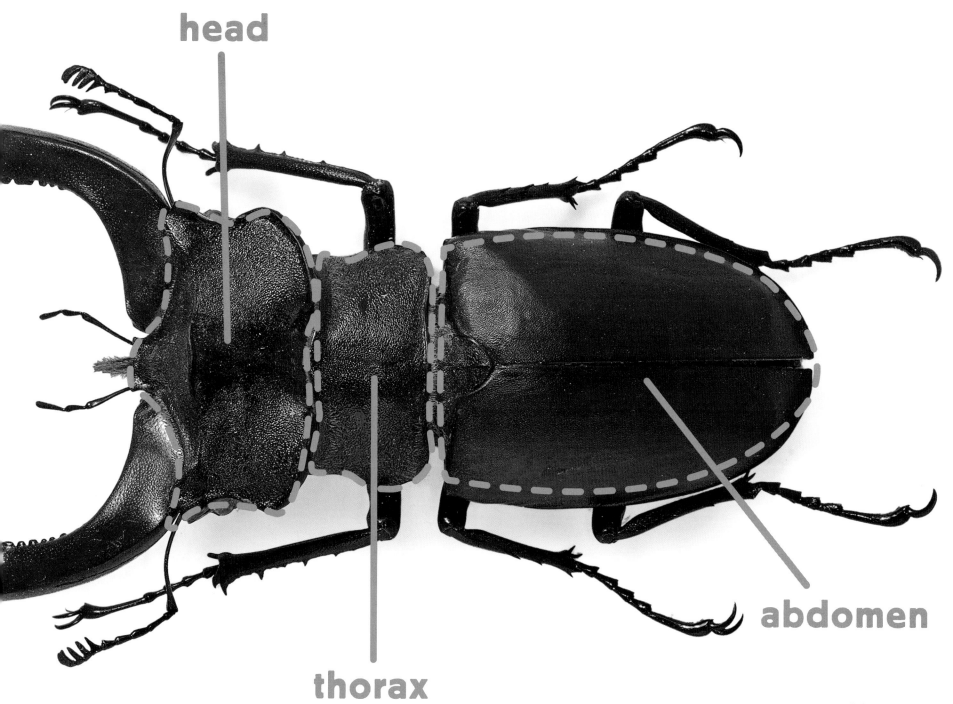

head

thorax

abdomen

11

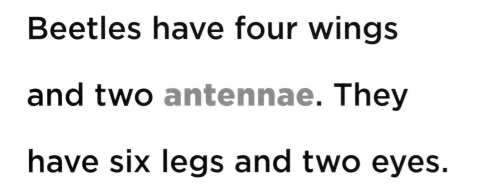

Beetles have four wings and two **antennae**. They have six legs and two eyes.

12

13

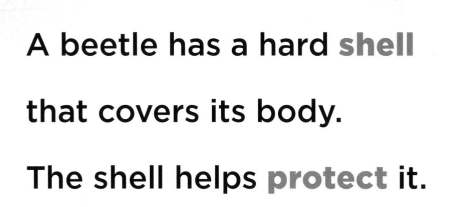

A beetle has a hard **shell** that covers its body.
The shell helps **protect** it.

15

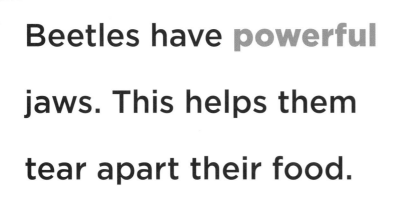

Beetles have **powerful** jaws. This helps them tear apart their food.

17

Food

Most beetles eat plant parts like leaves, fruit, and wood. Some beetles eat other insects or small animals.

18

Beetles Help the Earth

Beetles help break down
dead plants. Some beetles
move **pollen**, which helps
plants grow.

More Facts

- There are over 300,000 species of beetles known to scientists in the world.

- Scientists estimate there could actually be between 4 million and 8 million beetle species.

- Fireflies are beetles. They can glow in the dark!

Glossary

abdomen – the back part of an insect's body.

antennae – the two long, thin "feelers" on an insect's head.

pollen – the tiny, yellow grains of flowers.

powerful – strong.

protect – to keep safe.

thorax – the middle part of an insect's body.

Index

abdokids.com

Use this code to log on to abdokids.com and access crafts, games, videos and more!

Abdo Kids Code:

IBK0380